318
Patchwork
Patterns

First English edition published in 2014 by World Book Media, LLC

World Book Media LLC
134 Federal Street, Salem, MA 01970 USA
info@worldbookmedia.com

318 PATCHWORK PATTERNS
ISBN: 978-1-940552-11-8
Library of Congress Cataloging-in-Publication Data not available at time of printing

Originally published in Japanese language by EDUCATIONAL FOUNDATION BUNKA GAKUEN BUNKA PUBLISHING BUREAU
English edition published by arrangement with EDUCATIONAL FOUNDATION BUNKA GAKUEN BUNKA PUBLISHING BUREAU through The English Agency (Japan) Ltd.

Publisher: Sunao Onuma
Photography: Toshikatsu Watanabe
Art direction and design: Mihoko Amano
Pattern tracing: Satomi Dairaku
Production in cooperation with: Terue Uetake, Miyuki Ueno, Noriko Kijima, Yukari Namae, Hiroko Hakozaki, Kyoko Harada, Sumiko Bannai, Motoe Hukusato, Eriko Minamikawa, and NorikoYamada
Editor: Yoko Osawa (BUNKA PUBLISHING BUREAU)

English Editor: Lindsay Fair
Translation: Namiji Hatsuse

Printed in China
10 9 8 7 6 5 4 3 2 1

318 Patchwork Patterns

Original Patchwork and
Appliqué Designs by Kumiko Fujita

KUMIKO FUJITA

CONTENTS

INTRODUCTION

Over the course of my quilting career, I have explored a wide variety of themes. I spent an entire year fixated on floral motifs and even went through a phase where all I sewed were Christmas-inspired blocks. Though my subject matters have varied greatly, one element has remained constant: I always used the same techniques to construct my designs. In fact, patchwork and appliqué have been used by quilters for centuries, proving that these methods are truly timeless.

My favorite part of designing patchwork blocks is using simple shapes to create realistic-looking motifs. Fabric choice also plays a key role in the design of these blocks. Color and pattern add detail and dimension to a motif and influence the overall impression of a design. Don't be afraid to combine solids, stripes, polka dots, and plaids within a single block—you'll be surprised to learn that multiple prints can all work together harmoniously to create a truly dynamic design.

I first started quilting after discovering floral appliqué motifs at an antique quilt exhibit. Inspired by these traditional designs, I began drawing my own appliqué patterns. The appliqué blocks included in this book span 30 years of my work and range from simple, symmetrical wreaths to elaborate bouquets.

I hope you enjoy this collection of 318 block designs. Combine different motifs to construct a one-of-a-kind quilt or use these blocks as inspiration for your own creations. Happy quilting!

—Kumiko Fujita

PATCHWORK

Patchwork quilting has always held a certain allure for me: I love the way straight and simple pieces fit together just like a jigsaw puzzle. In my opinion, the most well-designed patterns use the fewest number of pieces possible to accurately represent a shape and are easy to sew.

When designing a block, I use a thick pencil and a ruler to draw my image out on a 6" × 6" (15 × 15 cm) square of graph paper. Then, I'll go back and erase unnecessary lines to simplify the design as much as possible.

Remember that straight lines work best for patchwork blocks. Circles can be replaced with hexagons and embroidery or appliqué can be used to complete small details.

Enjoy this collection of fun and festive patchwork motifs, or try your hand at designing your own blocks!

HOW TO USE THE PATCHWORK TEMPLATES

- The majority of patchwork templates in this book are 2 ³⁄₈" × 2 ³⁄₈" (6 × 6 cm).
- The number patchwork blocks on pages 51-52 are 2" × 2 ³⁄₈" (4.8 × 6 cm).
- The templates can be enlarged as desired. I recommend using a photocopier to enlarge the templates 250%. This will produce 6" × 6" (15 × 15 cm) finished blocks.

Sewing the Blocks

Special Note: The blocks in this book are designed for hand sewing. Certain blocks or sections are difficult to machine sew due to the small scale of the pieces or placement of the seams. However, you may be able to adapt these blocks to make them suitable for machine sewing by increasing the number of seams. If you plan to sew these blocks by machine, paper piecing works well.

1. Use a photocopier to enlarge the template to desired size.

2. Cut the paper template pieces out. Arrange the templates on the wrong side of your fabric and trace.

3. Add ³⁄₈" (0.8 cm) seam allowance to all piece edges and cut out the fabric.

4. Sew adjacent pieces with right sides together. Based on the design of the block, you may need to hand sew certain areas, especially if the pieces are small.

5. Press the seam allowances in the direction of the darker fabric.

6. Add any embroidered or appliquéd details to complete the block.

Sweets

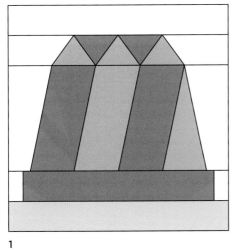

1

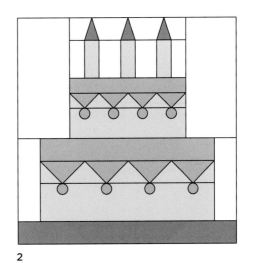

4

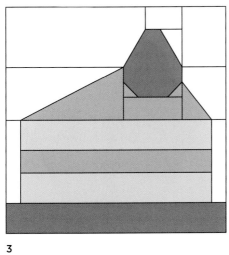

5

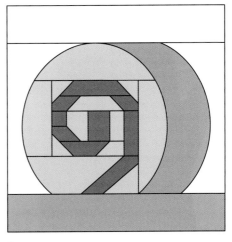

3

2

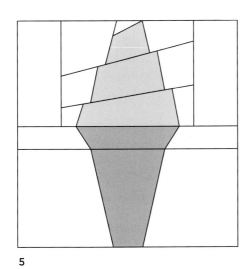

6

Tea Time

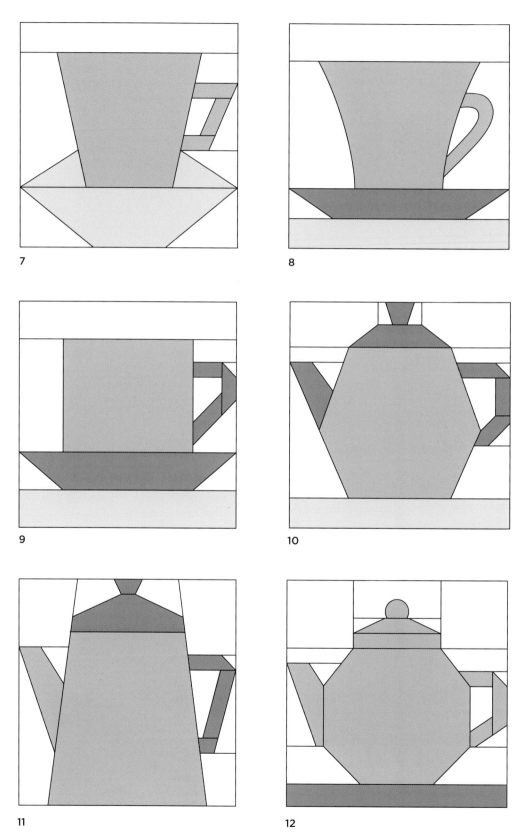

7

8

9

10

11

12

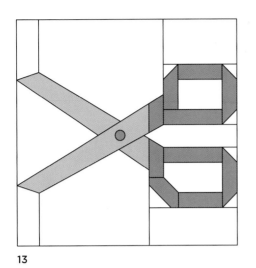

13

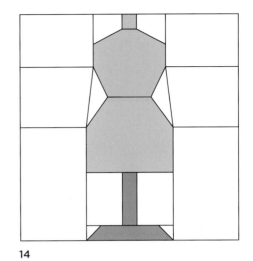

14

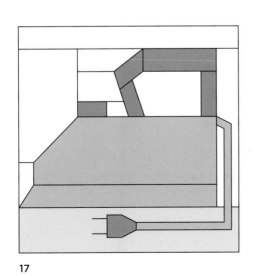

15

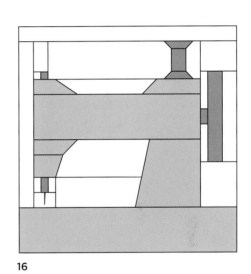

16

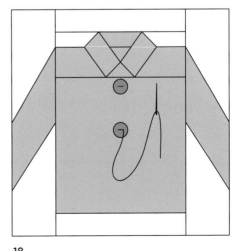

17

18

At the Circus

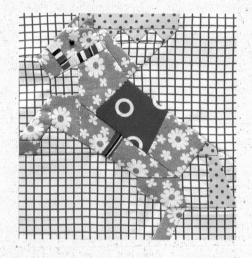

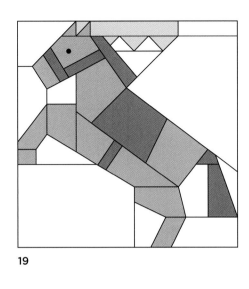

19

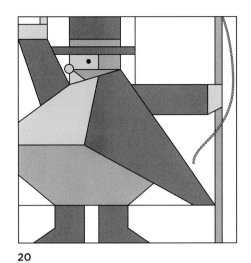

20

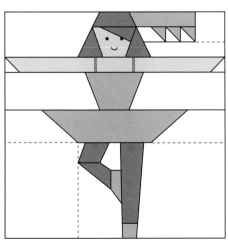

21

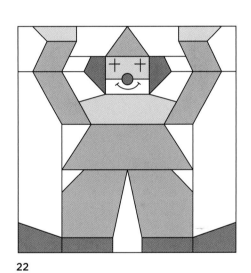

22

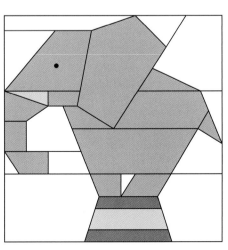

23 Note: If using a large print for the block background, do not cut along the dotted lines. Instead, cut large background pieces along solid lines only.

24

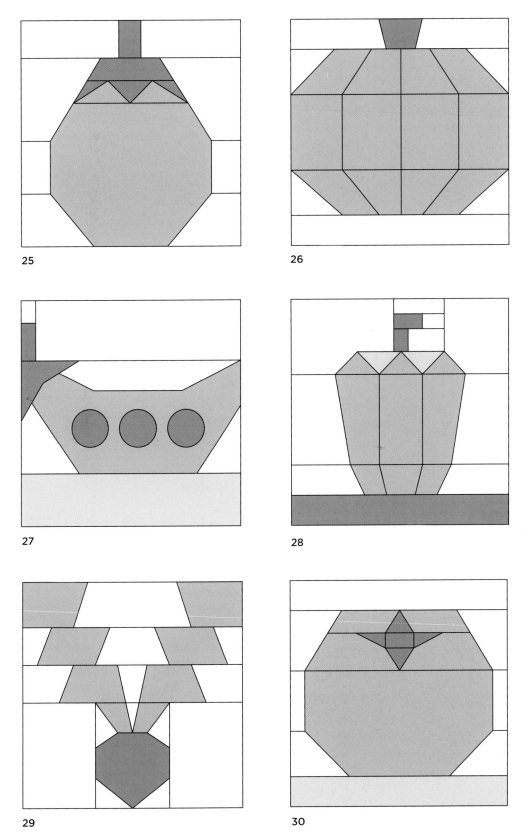

25

26

27

28

29

30

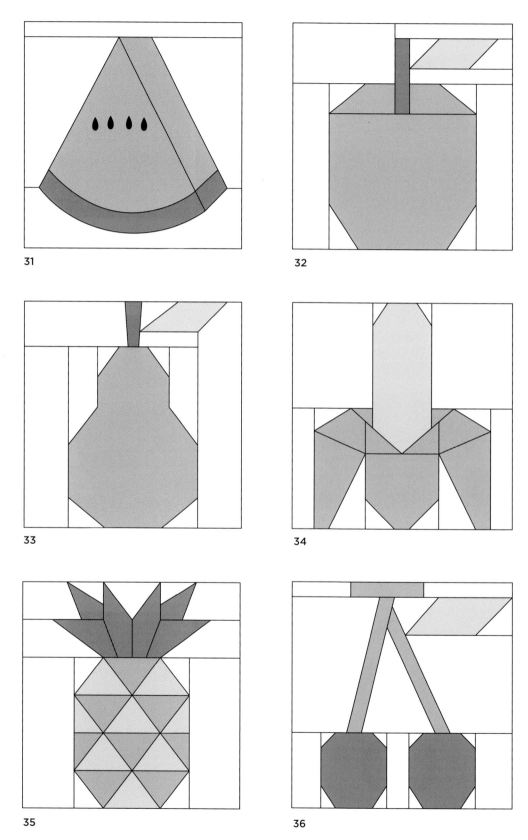

31

32

33

34

35

36

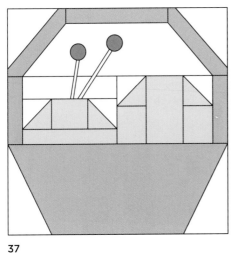

37

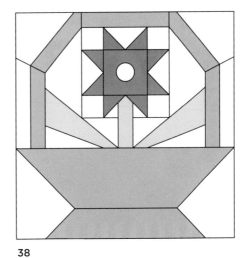

38

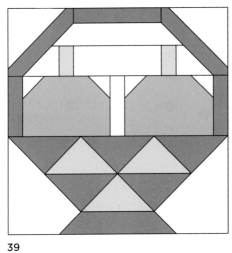

39

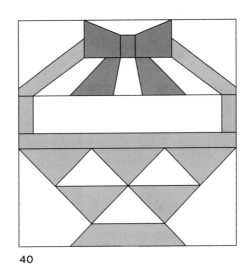

40

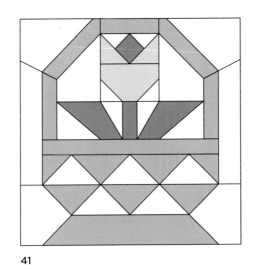

41

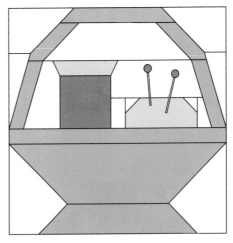

42

Vehicles

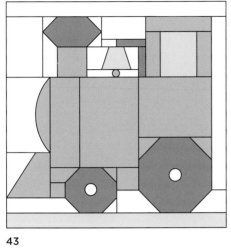

43

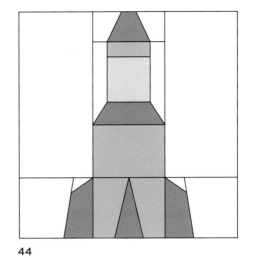

44

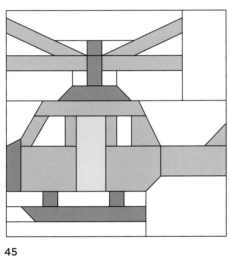

45

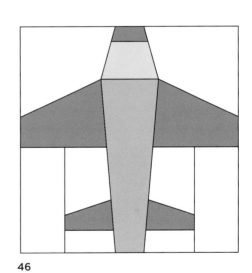

46

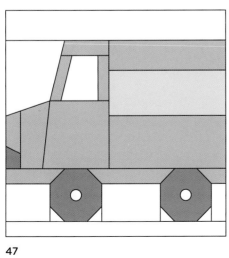

47

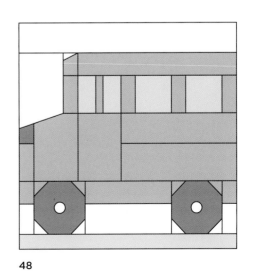

48

Girls' Night Out

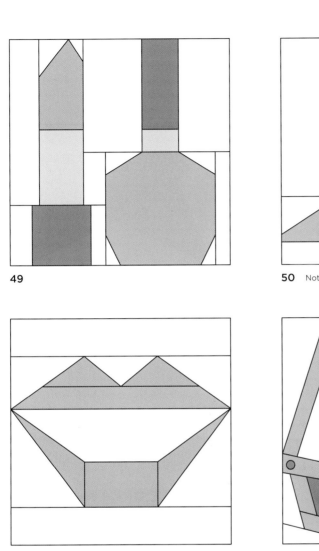

49

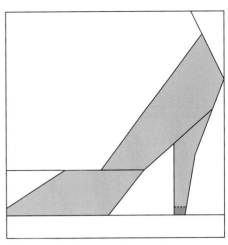

50 Note: Try a contrasting fabric for the tip of the heel.

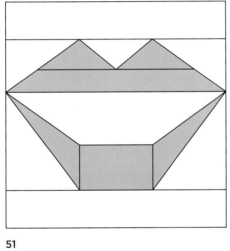

51

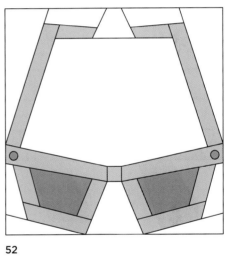

52

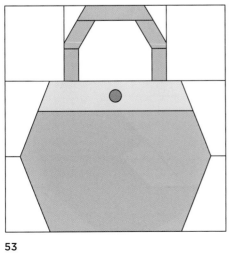

53

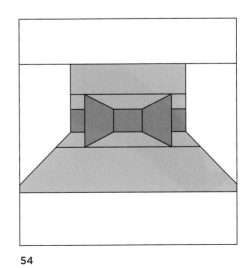

54

Rain or Shine

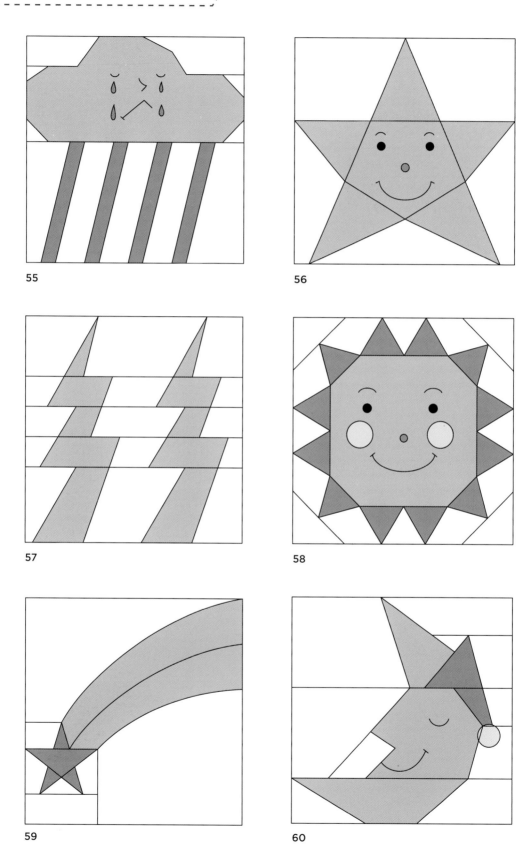

55

56

57

58

59

60

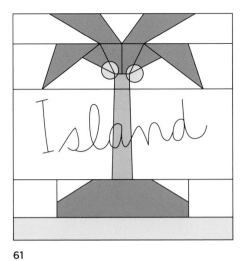

61

62

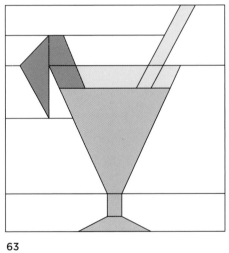

63

64

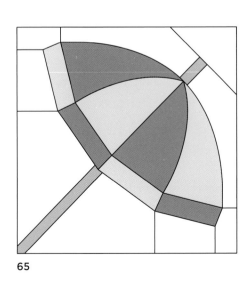

65

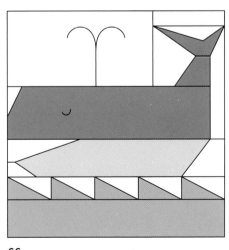

66

In the Kitchen

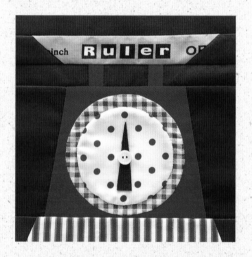

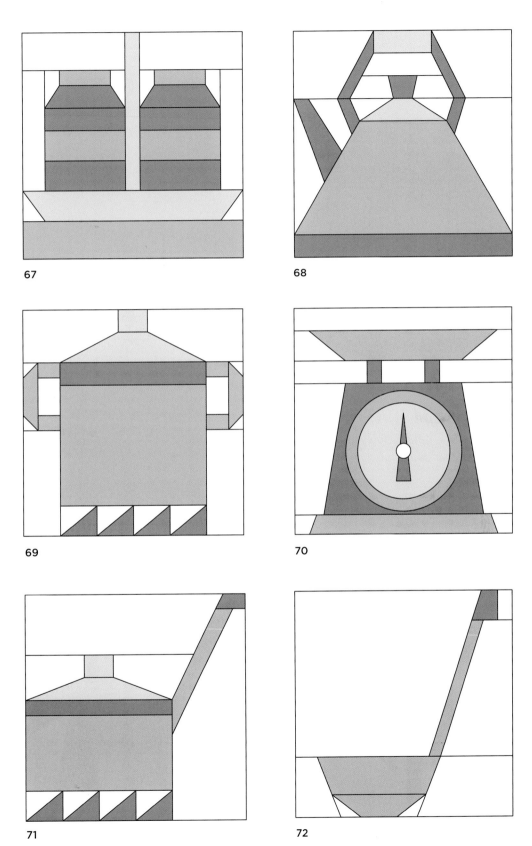

67

68

69

70

71

72

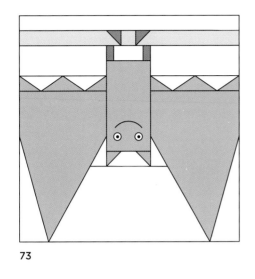

73

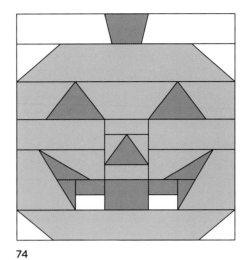

74

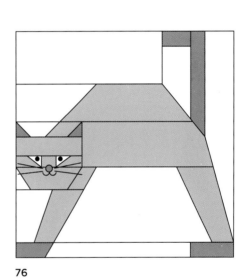

75

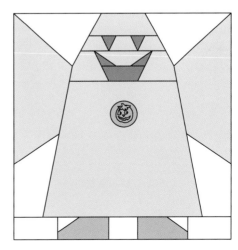

76

IT IS TIME TO SLEEP.

GOOD NIGHT.....

8am.–11pm.

77

78

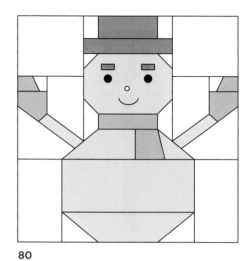

79

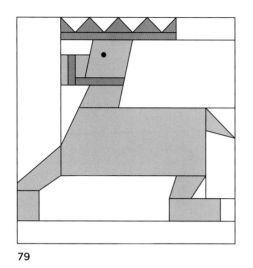

81

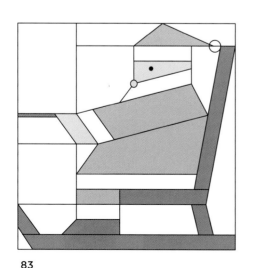

83

80

82

84

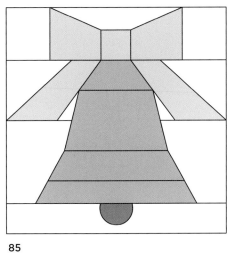

85

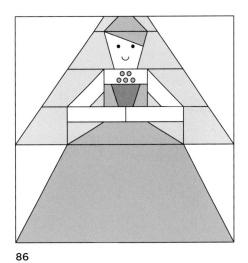

86

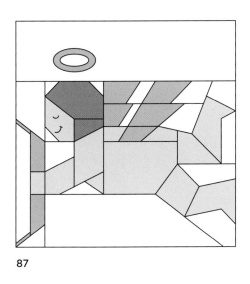

87

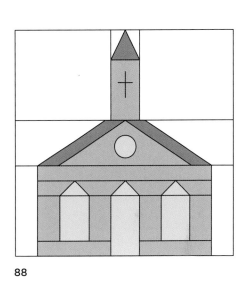

88

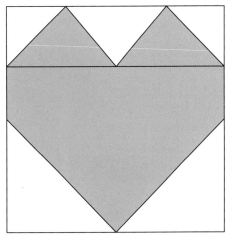

89

90

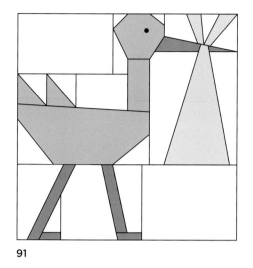

91

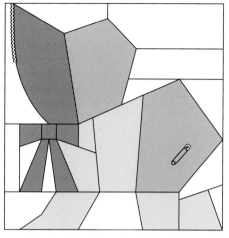

92

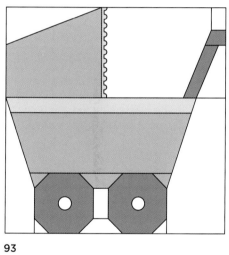

93

Baby's first...

94

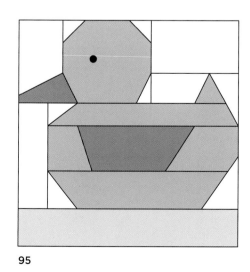

95

96

Down on the Farm

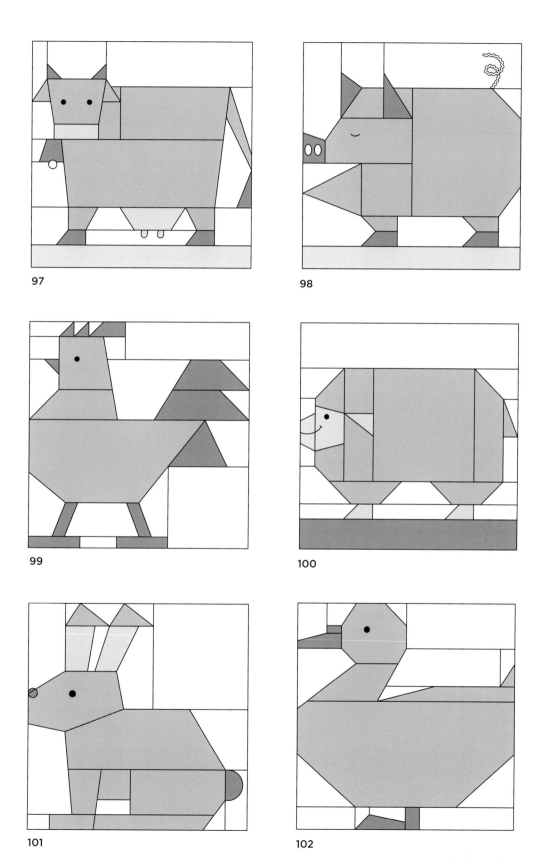

97

98

99

100

101

102

In the Garden

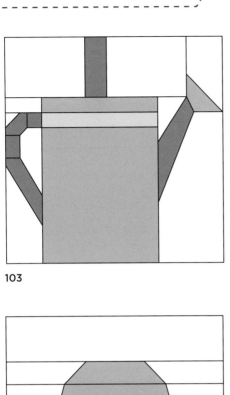

103

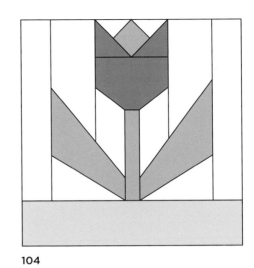

104

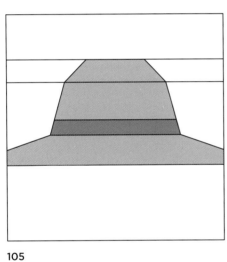

105

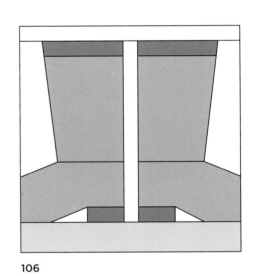

106

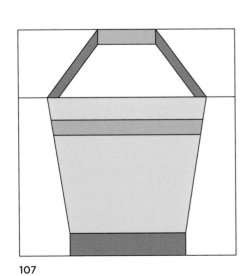

107

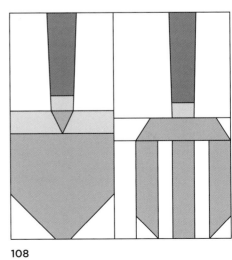

108

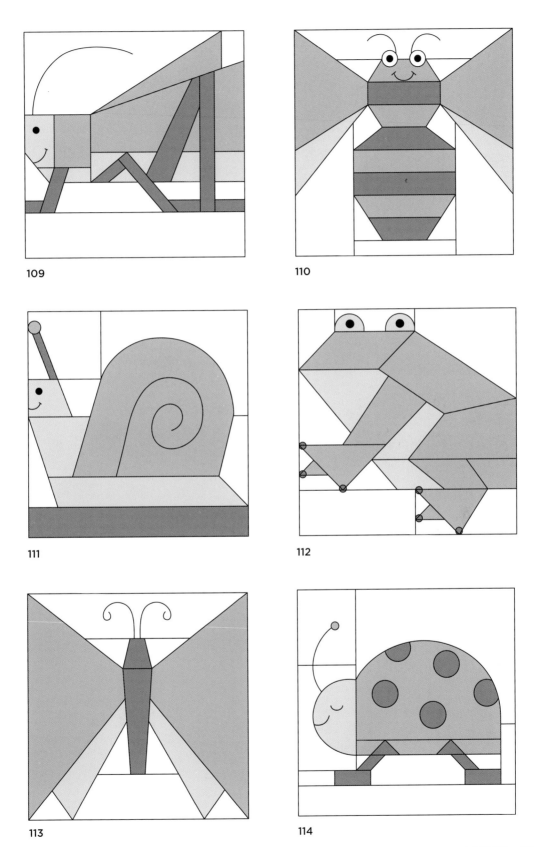

109

110

111

112

113

114

On the Water

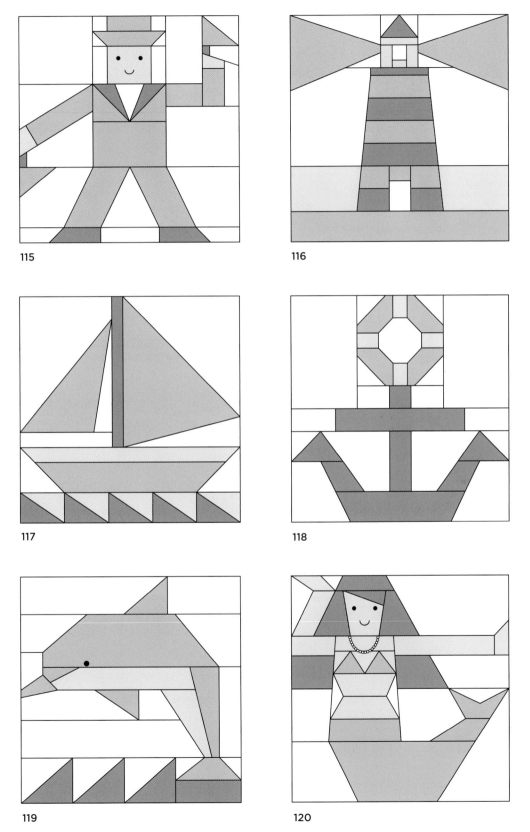

115

116

117

118

119

120

Toy Land

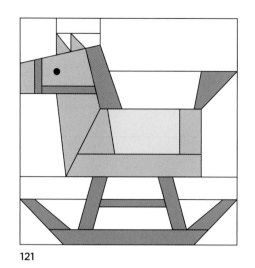

121

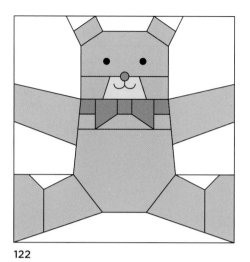

122

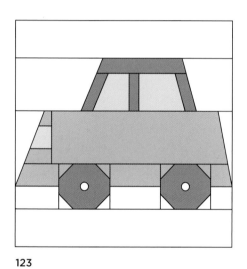

123

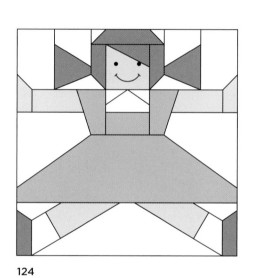

124

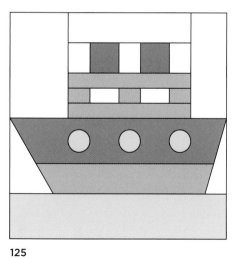

125

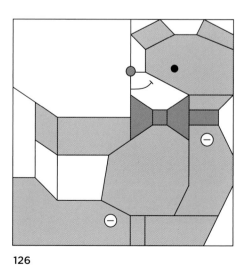

126

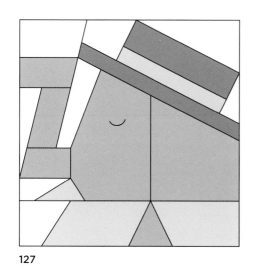

127

128

129

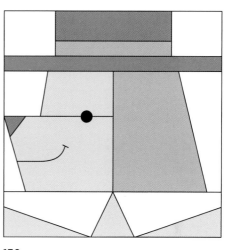

130

131

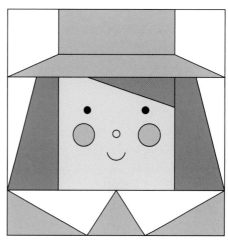

132

Dogs

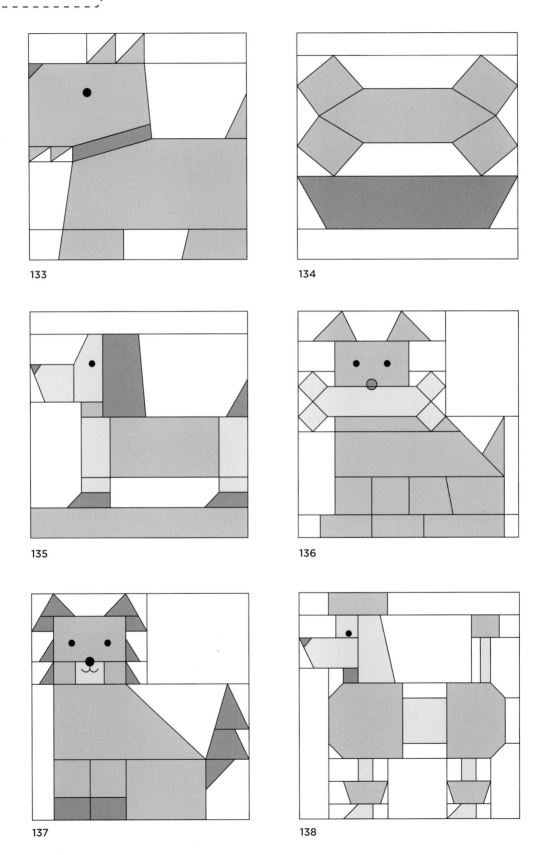

133

134

135

136

137

138

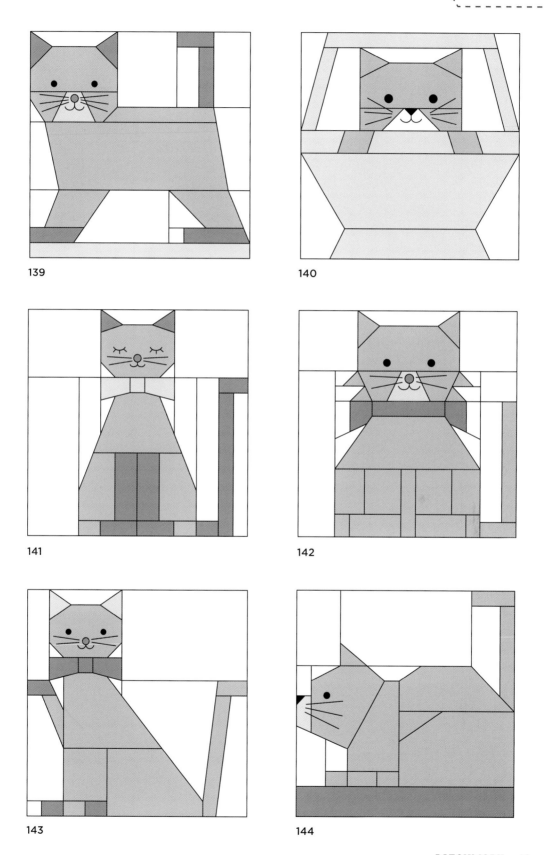

139

140

141

142

143

144

Birds

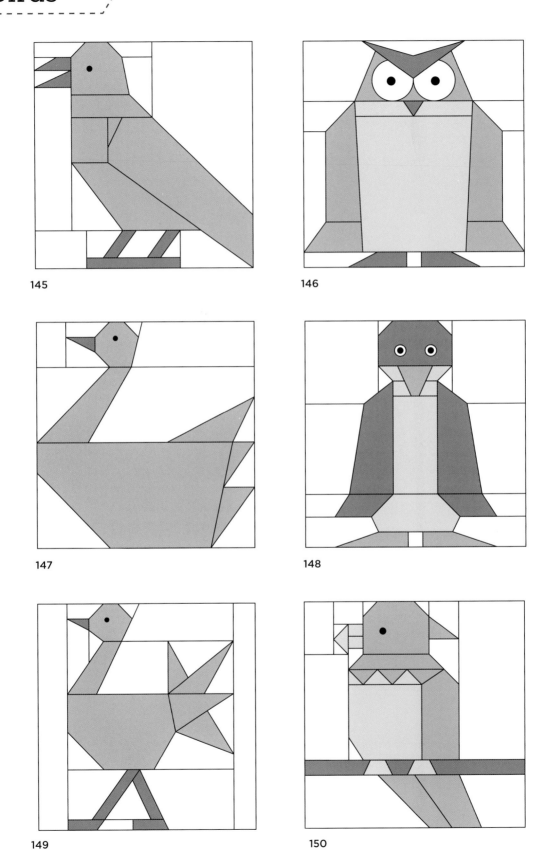

145

146

147

148

149

150

151

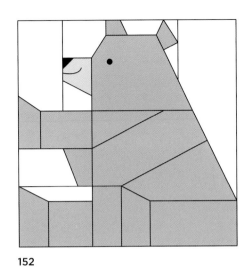

152

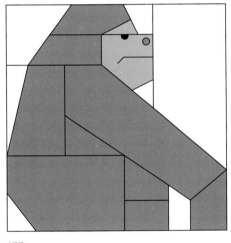

153

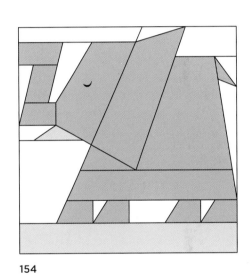

154

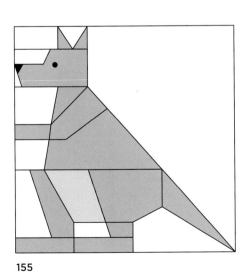

155

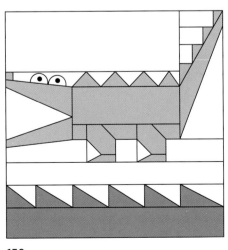

156

Home Sweet Home

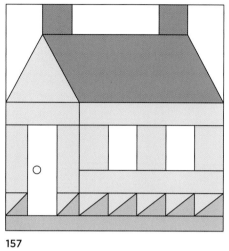

157

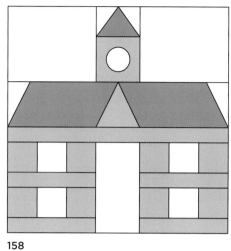

158

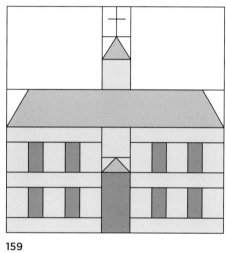

159

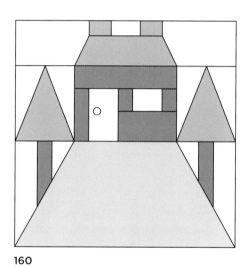

160

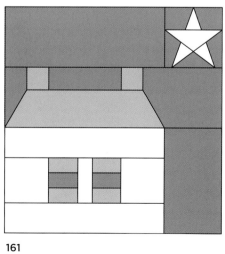

161

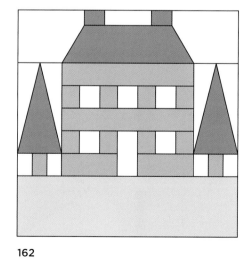

162

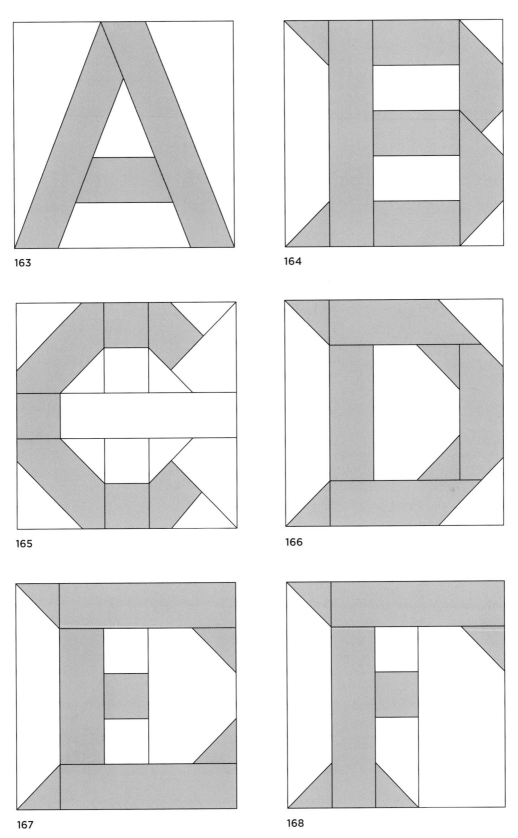

163

164

165

166

167

168

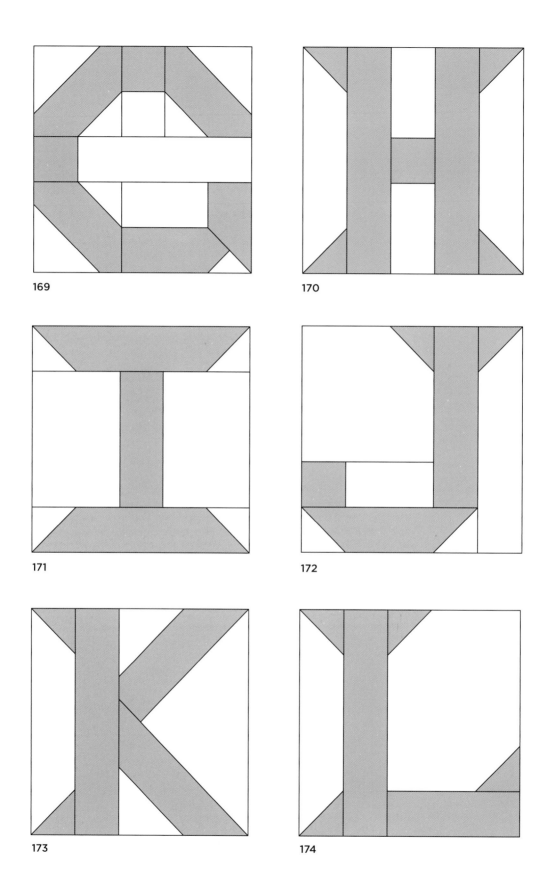

169

170

171

172

173

174

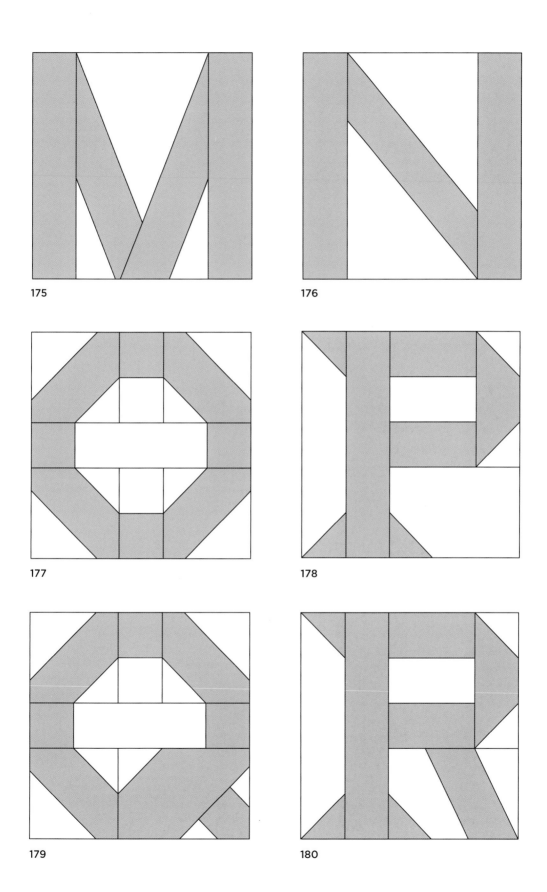

175

176

177

178

179

180

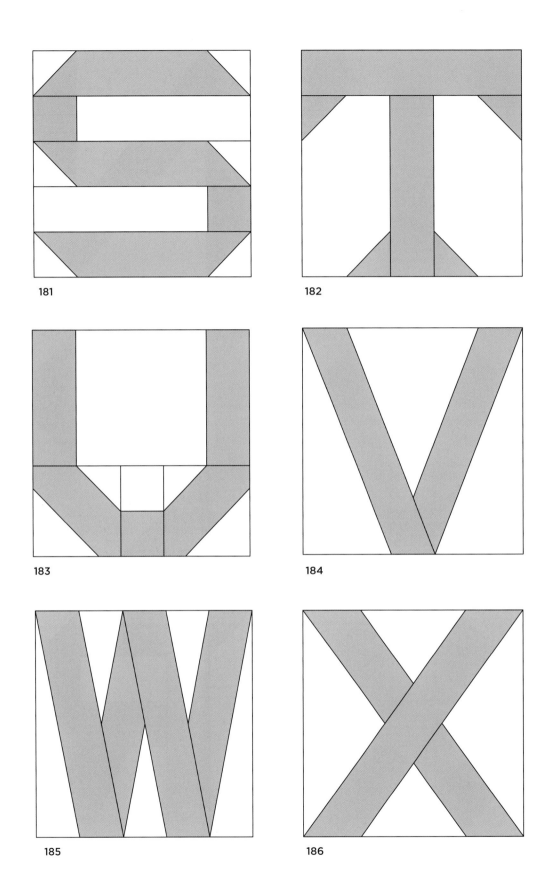

181

182

183

184

185

186

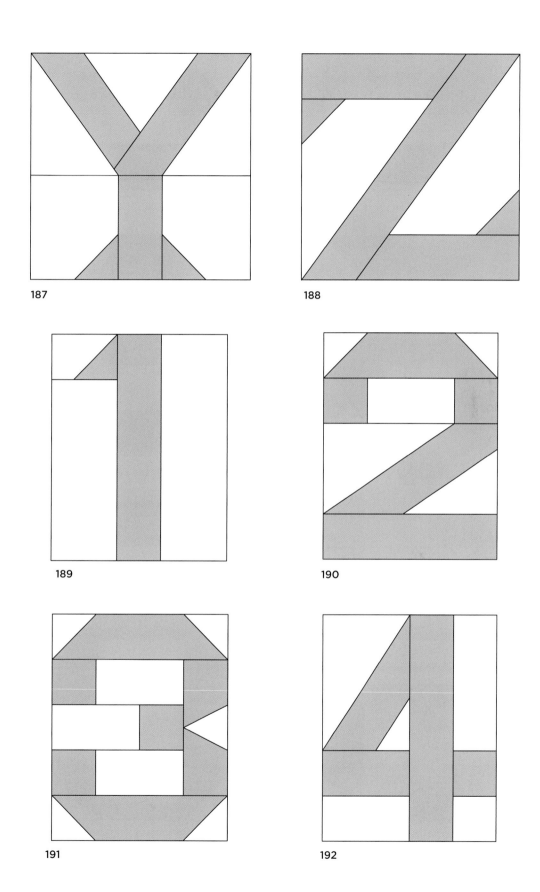

187

188

189

190

191

192

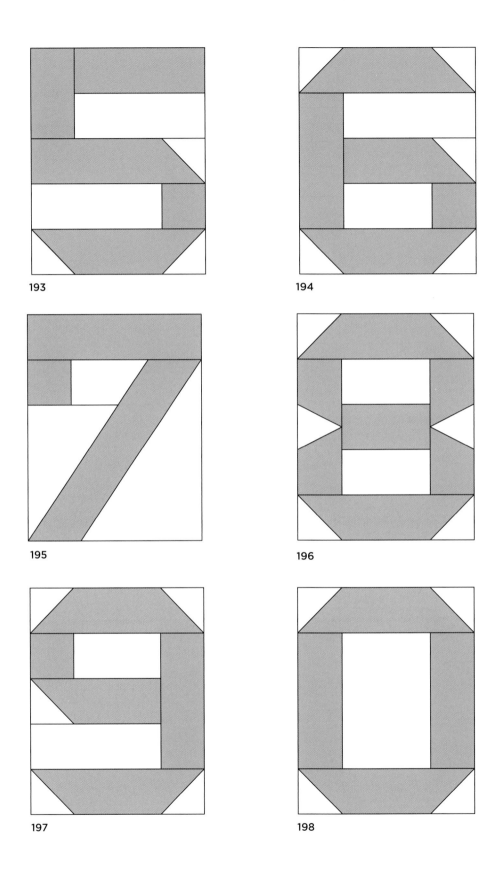

193

194

195

196

197

198

A NOTE ON FABRIC

One of the most common questions I am asked is: "Where did you get that fabric?" I feel bad when I have to tell a fellow quilter that it is no longer available. The truth is, I am a fabric collector. When I am in a store and see a fabric that I like, I always buy it, even if I don't have a specific need for it just yet. My philosophy is that it is better to just buy the fabric, otherwise, I will regret it later! Trust me, the time will come when you have the perfect use for that exact fabric.

In addition to traditional quilting cotton, I also incorporate vintage fabric and handkerchiefs into my work. Keep an eye out for fun prints at flea markets and antique shops so you can build your own stash.

Experiment with different colors and prints. I love florals, stripes, polka dots, and text...all combined in one block! I hope my fabric choices inspire you to step out of your comfort zone and expand your creative boundaries.

APPLIQUÉ

In contrast to patchwork, appliqué is all about soft curves and three-dimensional shapes. This collection of blocks includes two different styles of appliqué. The first half of the collection (pages 60-71) is comprised of my recent work and features simple shapes that were inspired by traditional appliqué motifs. The second half of the collection (pages 72-79) contains a few of my most popular appliqué motifs that were first introduced about 30 years ago. These designs are more detailed and complex, but they are timeless.

Have fun experimenting with different fabrics—try using felt, or combine high contrast colors such as red and black for bold blocks. See pages 56-59 for fabric and color combination ideas. These motifs can be combined to create wall hangings and quilts, or you can even use the templates for embroidery or quilting designs.

HOW TO USE THE APPLIQUÉ TEMPLATES

- The majority of appliqué templates in this book are 2 ³/₈" × 2 ³/₈" (6 × 6 cm).
- The fruit basket templates on page 79 are 3" x 3" (7.5 x 7.5 cm).
- The templates can be enlarged as desired. I recommend using a photo-copier to enlarge the templates 366%. This will produce 8 ³/₄" × 8 ³/₄" (22 × 22 cm) finished blocks.
- Use the templates as they appear, or create your own variations by mixing and matching different flower and leaf designs.

Sewing the Blocks

1. Transfer the appliqué block design to the right side of your base fabric.

2. Cut the paper template pieces out. Arrange the templates on the right side of your appliqué fabric and trace. Add ¹/₄" (0.4-0.5 cm) seam allowance to all piece edges and cut out the fabric.

3. Blind stitch the appliqué pieces to the base fabric, folding the seam allowance under as you work. For designs with multiple layers, appliqué the bottom layer to the base fabric first, then continue with subsequent layers.

> If you are using an appliqué fabric that does not fray, such as felt, you do not need to add seam allowance. Instead, you can cut the appliqué pieces out along the finishing lines and appliqué to the base fabric using blanket stitch or zigzag stitch.

When you use a muted color scheme, even contrasting
color combinations create a soft and calm look.

258

204

239

269

200

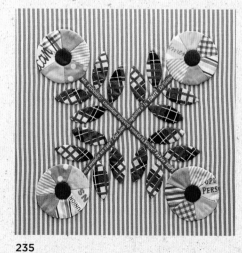

235

Strongly contrasting colors were used for these blocks.
The power of color is showcased in these vivid designs.

209

252

257

238

202

259

All of these blocks share a pink and black color scheme. When a design has a cohesive color scheme, it is easy to combine stripes, dots, and checkered patterns effectively.

237

203

262

206

254

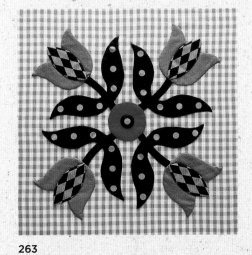

263

These blocks are composed entirely of red, white, and black fabrics.
Using fewer colors within a design creates a bold and modern look.

213

218

219

267

208

255

Classic Flowers

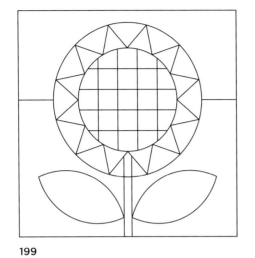

199

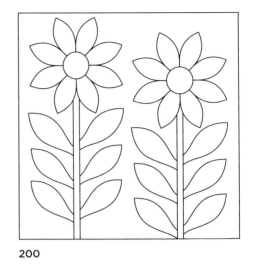

200

201

202

203

204

205

206

207

208

209

210

Wreaths

211

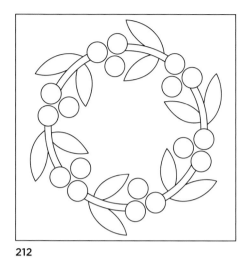

212

213

214

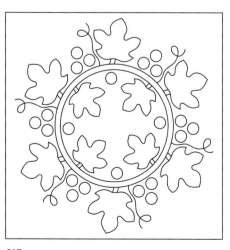

215

216

217 First construct the flowers using patchwork, then appliqué to complete.

218

219

220

The roses
are in full
bloom now

221

222

Oak Leaves

223

224

225

226

227

228

229

230

231

232

233

234

Circles

235

236

237

238

239

240

241

242

243

244

245

246

Love Birds

247

248

249

250

251

252

253

254

255

256

257

258

Tulips

259

260

261

262

263

264

265

266

267

268

269

270

Basic Baskets

For all blocks: First construct the basket using patchwork, then appliqué to complete.

271

272

273

274

275

276

277

278

279

280

281

282

Festive Florals

283

284

285

286

287

288

289

290

291

292

293

294

Hawaiian Garlands

295

296

297

298

299

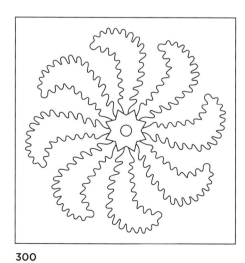

300

301

302

303

304

305

306

Flower Baskets

307

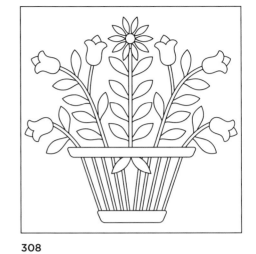

308

309

310

311

312

313

314

315

316

317

318

ABOUT THE AUTHOR

A native of Tokyo, Japan, Kumiko Fujita began her creative career in the field of graphic design. Fujita's love of color, text, and print influences her current work as a fabric and patchwork designer. She is known for her whimsical, fresh, and fun design aesthetic. She currently designs a fabric line called First of Infinity and is the author of multiple books in Japan. To learn more about Kumiko Fujita, visit her website: http://www.quiltersstudio.jp

PROFILE

KUMIKO FUJITA

Looking for more original *Japanese* quilting projects in English?

Zakka Workshop Patterns

Quick and easy patchwork patterns for cute home and fashion accessories.

Yoko Saito Patterns

Patchwork and appliqué patterns designed by renowned quilter Yoko Saito.

Find these patterns and other designs at your favorite local quilt shop or online at:
https://www.etsy.com/shop/ZakkaWorkshopStore

worldbookmedia
www.worldbookmedia.com